YOU CAN TEI YOU'RE A CHARLOTTEAN IF...

YOU CAN TELL YOU'RE A CHARLOTTEAN IF...

by
Margaret Bigger
&
Betsy Webb

Illustrated by Loyd Dillon

ABB

A. Borough Books

ISBN   0-9640606-6-3

Library of Congress Catalog Card Number 98-71923

Printed in the United States of America

Cover design by Loyd Dillon
Illustrations by Loyd Dillon

aBb

A. Borough Books
P.O. Box 15391
Charlotte NC 28211

PREFACE

Soon after Susan Webb from York, Pennsylvania called each of us to suggest that we collaborate on this book, cute endings were popping into our heads to complete the sentence, "You know you're from Charlotte if..."

When we mentioned the idea to friends and acquaintances, they would quickly say, "Be sure to include..." or "Don't forget..." It soon became apparent, though, that we must add a section referring to longtime Charlotteans and one for newcomers. Margaret was hearing from mostly natives; Betsy was talking with people who were new to town. Their perspectives were entirely different. Meanwhile, we decided on the title, *You Can Tell You're a Charlottean If...* When Susan heard that we had changed the name, she was distressed. "Please don't use that word, 'Charlottean,'" she pleaded. "My friends say it sounds too much like 'charlatan.'"

We got a hearty laugh out of that and assured her that those of us who live here are used to being called "Charlotteans." The people of Charlotte are good-hearted genuine, generous Southerners, whether homegrown or transplants. We **like** to poke fun at ourselves. Proof: the long list of contributors to this book.

And after you've read this volume, kindly send us **your** endings for our next one!

ACKNOWLEDGMENTS

Although many of the lines are our own, we simply could not have had a book which represented points of view from a variety of geographic areas in and around Charlotte without the help of *The Charlotte Observer*, specifically the Mecklenburg Neighbors section.

We are especially grateful to Pat Borden Gubbins, who wrote two fine articles, and editors Nancy Webb, Cliff Harrington and Frank Barrows, who endorsed and encouraged the project. We were delighted with the Al Phillips cartoon, which captured the spirit of fun we all have when we can admit our own quirks.

We also thank John Hancock, who surprised us by devoting one of his shows on WBT to call-ins on our topic and sending us a tape of the responses.

In both cases, however, it was Charlotte residents who supplied the lines that made us chuckle or react with a "I didn't know that!" "Oh, wow!" or "Say WHAT?" Many people sent in official entries or handed us their favorite lines. These are listed among our contributors. But there are many more who, by stopping us in public to suggest an idea, gave us a thought which germinated later on paper. You know who you are. We may have forgotten, if we ever knew, your name. But we want you to know that we are grateful to you as well.

LIST OF CONTRIBUTORS

Bet Ancrum
Chuck Barnes
Anilee Lewis Bateman
Jean Beatty
Jane Bennett
Wade Best
Randy Bigger
Julia Bing
David Boggs
Donna Brim
Punkin Brookshire
Gwen Brown
Lynda Burch
Joy Burton
Joseph E. Caldwell
Phil Clutts

Mike Cozza
Bill Curry
Sarah Dagenhart
Carolyn Davenport
Maureen S. Davis
Diane Davis
Loyd Dillon
Betty Zane Dover
Pamela Duvick
Larry M. Efird
Stan Elrod
Dana Ernsberger
Chris Folk
Colleen Furr
Ann Wright Galant
Paul H. Hailey, Sr.

John Hancock
Stephanie Hardy
Ken Harrison, Sr.
Lucy Harrison
Memory Honeycutt
Jack Horan
Macee Hough
Jane Howard
Gloria Hutchins
John Jones
Jimmy Kilgo
Lori E. Krimminger
Bob Kumerow
Lynn Lee
Gray Little
Thomas R. Lloyd

LIST OF CONTRIBUTORS

Peggy Cope Lyerly
John Lynch
Glenda Warren Lynch
Ray Martin
Jim Martin
Bren Martin
Katherine McAdams
Ethel McMillan
Freda Montgomery
Joy Moore
Gregory Lee Moore
Walter S. Morton
Mickey Neal
Dolores Nixon
John Offerdahl

Florine Olive
Roger Palmer
D'Arlene Pound
Dannye Romine Powell
Buddy Reid
Joe Robinson
Leonard Robinson
Amy Rogers
Sandy Roork
Jatana Royster
Jay Rubin
Hope Schene
Tara Servatius
Ruth Silverman
Sam Sloan

James Smith, Jr.
Vicky Shoemaker Smith
Sherri Smith
Susan Spaugh
Jack Starnes
Paul M. Visser
Bob Welsh
Bill White
Nancy Whitehurst
Butch Wilburn
Elizabeth K. Williams
Ann Williams
Allison Kratt Winiker
Linda Walker Wooten

CONTENTS

YOU'RE A CHARLOTTEAN IF...

Genu-wine Generalities

Test yourself. See if you fit the profile of a typical Charlottean. Here's how. You can tell you're a Charlottean if...

You have Billy Graham tapes in your glove compartment and Jack Daniel's under your seat.

You put out pine needles for your bushes, a basketball goal for your kids and beer for the slugs.

You get a paycheck from—and/or owe—NationsBank, First Union or Wachovia.

YOU'RE A CHARLOTTEAN IF...

You own a four-wheel-drive vehicle, although we average less than one snow day per year.

Your garage also holds a pickup, if a male over 18 lives at your place.

Your child spends more time on a school bus than in any of his classes.

You consider the greatest advantage of living in Fourth Ward is a free uptown parking space.

You can go to the Square, a Panthers game and your neighborhood shopping center and never see anyone you know.

YOU'RE A CHARLOTTEAN IF...

Your neighbors move away before you learn their names.

The building you work in has been razed and replaced at least once.

No three children in your neighborhood go to the same school.

You've got goose droppings on your front porch, lawn and favorite golf course.

You have to change buses uptown to get anywhere.

It seems perfectly normal to go to the mall to ice skate.

YOU'RE A CHARLOTTEAN IF...

You cheer for the "hottest" dance band in town: the Johnson C. Smith University marching band.

When you refer to UCLA, you mean "University of Charlotte, 'Lizabeth Avenue."

You're watching a high school play, and the entire cast has pierced body parts.

You can identify the caricatures of locals at the Palm Restaurant—or better yet, at the Blue Marlin.

You know that a buttercup is *not* a yellow daffodil—it's spelled with a capital B and can be found in the 300 block of Providence Road.

YOU'RE A CHARLOTTEAN IF...

The only cows your children have seen are at Ben & Jerry's.

You know in your heart of hearts that people on the other side of the planet will not be referring to Charlotte as a "world class city" any time soon.

You're envious of the largest metropolis south of here, so you want Charlotte to grow—"but not like Atlanta!"

You're sure that the Raptor Center has absolutely nothing to do with religious or sexual ecstasy.

Even your older children know that the Briarhoppers aren't rabbits.

YOU'RE A CHARLOTTEAN IF...

You call the uptown thoroughfare "Trine Street."

You stress the first syllable of many words: *um*brella, *Thanks*giving, *fi*nance, *po*lice and *Mon*roe.

You don't conjugate the verb to come. You just use the present tense.

You're not perturbed to see signs with plurals spelled with "'s."

Like the street-sign makers, you can't spell anyway. Or you spell the same name more creatively every block.

YOU'RE A CHARLOTTEAN IF...

Your sentence doesn't start with "Where I come from..."

You have a habit of saying, "We don't *care* how they do it up North" to anyone without a Southern accent.

When you hear "Bless your heart," you brace for criticism.

As a working woman uptown, you are smartly dressed above the ankles and wear dirty tennis shoes below.

No matter how great your qualifications, you haven't a chance of becoming governor of this state.

YOU'RE A CHARLOTTEAN IF...

You know at least three bank presidents by first name, sight or idiosyncracies.

You declare your independence by parking your pickup *in front of* your condo.

You avoid the longest line at the coliseum. For barbecue? Nope. ATM machine.

In March, you expect a snowstorm and a heat wave.

You'd volunteer for anything except the fire department.

You appreciate Charlotte for what it IS rather than whining about what it's NOT.

YOU'RE A CHARLOTTEAN IF...

A Colorful City!

We like to think we are colorblind, but maybe we see colors a bit differently. You might, too, because you can tell you are a Charlottean if...

Your fender is decorated with orange barrel paint.

You're aware that the world's largest green jukebox was built by First Union.

You know what people are talking about when they mention the "big pink church."

YOU'RE A CHARLOTTEAN IF...

You find out that the "green & white construction company"—which takes more time, uses more people and makes more messes than its counterparts—is run by the city.

You are surrounded by true blue fanatics (especially evident on Duke-Carolina game days).

Meanwhile, even when cloudy, the sky is always Carolina blue.

Your kids' most used school playground is yellow and on wheels.

You're frequently covered in black and blue but are not hurt.

YOU'RE A CHARLOTTEAN IF...

You notice that stores sell more purple and teal *everything* here than in any other city.

You stomp the pedal to the metal when the traffic light's already yellow. (Virginians call that color "Carolina green.")

Those of you who live near Lake Norman or Lake Wylie have orange toenails four months out of the year.

Your neck is redder than the dirt in your garden.

YOU'RE A CHARLOTTEAN IF...

A Tourist Town?

You may not be able to fathom why tourists come to your hometown, but you have some inside information they might find interesting or even helpful—because you're a Charlottean if...

You can't find a historic site to visit, but you can read about it on the marker in front of the parking lot where it used to be.

The road you frequently travel changes name seven times before you get to your destination.*

*Route 4: Billy Graham Parkway, Woodlawn Road, Runnymede Lane, Sharon Road, Wendover Road, Eastway Drive, Sugar Creek Road.

YOU'RE A CHARLOTTEAN IF...

You're aware that the second largest "downtown" area in the state (second only to Charlotte's) is SouthPark. But here's the "kicker:" You can only go uptown in Charlotte, because there *is no* downtown.

You would not head south—or north, for that matter—on Highway 21 to get to any of the four South 21 restaurants.

You've been here 10 years and you're *still* lost on the Queens Roads.

You don't have to be told that Myers Park High School is not really in Myers Park, neither Providence Day nor Providence High are on Providence Road, and Charlotte Country Day is not in the country.

YOU'RE A CHARLOTTEAN IF...

You can locate East, South and West Boulevard standing in one place, but you'll never find North Boulevard.

You know every possible way to get to Myrtle Beach—and where all the speed traps are along the way.

You can't get from Point A to Point B as the crow flies, if said points are more than .4 of a mile apart.

You know to say "Concord" like the airplane not the past act of conquering, but you pronounce Mooresville, Huntersville and Cherryville "Mooresvull," "Huntersvull" and "Churrvull."

YOU'RE A CHARLOTTEAN IF...

You think that Dallas is less than 20 miles away and Denver's near Lake Norman.

You have to *tell* visitors about the city's most elegant historic homes, because they've all been torn down.

You've always wondered what's on the plaque in the middle of the Square but don't want to get killed finding out.

Although you're not in Charlottesville, Virginia, you can easily find the Rotunda and Monticello near SouthPark.*

* The Rotunda Building houses offices and a restaurant on Congress Street. Morrison Regional Library on Morrison Boulevard is strikingly reminiscent of Thomas Jefferson's home, but Harris Teeter and Borders in Morrocroft Village have rotundas, too.

YOU'RE A CHARLOTTEAN IF...

You can look a stranger in the eye and insist that both I-77 and I-85 are north-south freeways.

Never mind the tourists, you want the Carolina Theater restored for the city—that is, our children—okay, for your own nostalgia's sake.

You give directions with turns where landmarks *used* to be. (A newcomer gets even by telling you to turn where things are *going* to be.)

YOU'RE A CHARLOTTEAN IF...

Traffic, Traffic, Traffic!

To hear them talk, residents, it seems, love Charlotte but hate traffic. So should we outlaw wheeled vehicles? Until then, you can tell you're a Charlottean if...

You're feeling guilty about sneaking under a changing red light and look in the rear view mirror to see two more cars run the signal.

Detour and one-lane-only signs always seem to divert *your* lane.

You never use your blinkers.

YOU'RE A CHARLOTTEAN IF...

While you and a whole line of traffic wait and then slowly ease up to the construction blockade in the center lane, *one, two and more* cars roar by your right side and merge way ahead of everyone else.

You try to be courteous and leave two car lengths ahead of you, but three cars swerve into the space.

You'd rather eat liver than drive down Independence Boulevard during rush hour.

You really don't believe them when they tell you the outer belt will be finished someday.

31

YOU'RE A CHARLOTTEAN IF...

You find yourself passing more cars on the right than on the left.

The driver behind you blows his horn before the light turns green.

The young woman in front of you is smoking, putting on makeup and rearranging her hair, with one hand on the wheel from time to time.

A li'l ole lady in her oversized car is sitting halfway into your lane as she waits to come out of a side street.

A guy is turning toward you with a phone in one hand, pen in the other and mouth running full throttle.

YOU'RE A CHARLOTTEAN IF...

You park in the fire lane, ignoring the "no parking" sign.

You have taken driving lessons at the Charlotte Motor Speedway (the Richard Petty Driving Experience) to learn how to go 165 mph—and practice every chance you get.

This is the only city you know that has candid cameras—in bullet-proof boxes, yet—trained on your tail. Oh, but did you hear? While photographing red-light-runners, they ran out of film the first hour of the first day!

You are among the hundreds of residents who, after being told by radio and newspaper reports where the speed traps were located, had to pay a speeding ticket.

YOU'RE A CHARLOTTEAN IF...

Fanatic Fans? Who, Us?

They said an NBA team franchise would put us on the map, but it took an NFL, ECHL, WBA and the teaser of a MLB team to keep outsiders from mistaking Charlotte for Charlottesville, Virginia or Charleston, South Carolina. That's reason enough for our fervor. That's why you're definitely a Charlottean if...

You were incensed in 1986 when the Phoenix newspaper said that the only franchise Charlotte would get would have golden arches.

You are convinced that UNC-Chapel Hill has been afraid to schedule UNC-Charlotte in basketball—and for good reason.

YOU'RE A CHARLOTTEAN IF...

You are a Presbyterian, Baptist or Sunday Panthers fan.

You've admired the finest crystal chandelier in the area—at the Speedway.

You really get a bang out of watching hornets sting bulls, bucks and hawks.

You've seen insects wearing Alexander Julian outfits.

You're still asking "Zo who?"

You've 'bout stopped saying "How 'bout them Panthers?!"

YOU'RE A CHARLOTTEAN IF...

You question the wisdom of portraying an ever-changing cast of characters on the First Union mural, but you love it anyway.

Your pop took you to Checkers games when you were in diapers, and now you're a big fan again.

You know that Duke Power doesn't refer to basketball superiority.

You're dismayed that coliseum parking costs as much as lunch and stadium parking can be as high as an expense-account dinner.

You have a framed portrait of Dale Earnhardt or Jeff Gordon in your bedroom.

YOU'RE A CHARLOTTEAN IF...

You'd rather give big bucks (and even go into debt) to support sports instead of a symphony orchestra.

While awaiting the naming of the new basketball facility, you worried that Mike Cozza's prediction might be right: it could be called the Swisher Bowl.

You think it's cute to see a nut running around at the Charlotte Motor Speedway, because he's just a big lug anyway.

You don't have to revert to medieval times to see a dancing dragon.

You don't expect Chubby Checker to sing.

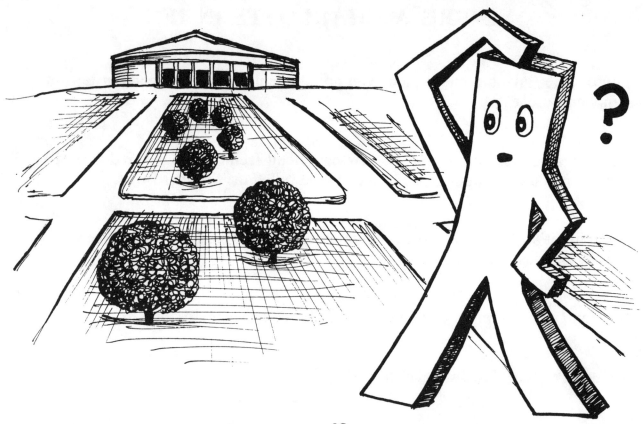

38

YOU'RE A CHARLOTTEAN IF...

No matter how close the score is, you leave a Hornets game before the last three game minutes to beat the traffic.

You took sides in the most bizarre sports contest ever—between leafy balls and the "Headless Gumby."

Your underwear has bugs on it.

YOU'RE A CHARLOTTEAN IF...

Eager Eaters, too!

Yep, we do like to feed our faces. Ever noticed all the obese people in shorts at Charlotte Knights baseball games? Anyway, you can tell you're a Charlottean if...

You put ketchup on your meat loaf, barbecue, chit'lin's and quiche. (Charlotte's the Ketchup Capital of the World, you know.)

You're in a Japanese restaurant eating sushi and watching NASCAR on TV.

You wouldn't be shocked to find a kitchen sink on a Wolfman's or Picasso's pizza.

YOU'RE A CHARLOTTEAN IF...

To obey the rules, you hold your business lunch meeting while still standing in line outside Lupie's Cafe.

You're not surprised when the *waitpersons* sing for your supper at Bravo!

You recall that, only a few years ago, one of the best restaurants in town went by the name of a slimy, disgusting mollusk (Slug's).

You've heard that Dikadee (as in Dikadee's Deli) is the name that Nick Collias used to call his baby brother George. George?

You know to order a cherry lemon Sprite at South 21.

43

YOU'RE A CHARLOTTEAN IF...

You salt your watermelon (cantaloupe, too).

You like peanuts in your Coke.

You keep enough Spam in the cupboard to last awhile.

You ask for liver mush at every Greek-owned restaurant, even the pancake house.

You can't stand runny grits or gritty mashed potatoes.

You would willingly eat at a place named for a cricket, panda or porcupine.

YOU'RE A CHARLOTTEAN IF...

You couldn't figure out why Honda would sell food, until you found out it was a Japanese restaurant, not a car dealership.

You are delighted that most mom-and-pop restaurateurs nowadays have unpronounceable foreign names.

Despite your anti-alcohol upbringing, you have to admit that liquor-by-the-drink has brought in more varieties of foods than beverages.

YOU'RE A CHARLOTTEAN IF...

Okay, We're a Bit Wacky.

If you are, too, you'll fit right in. Yep, you know you're a Charlottean if...

You think honeybees live in hornets' nests and hornets work in a hive.

Your oak trees wear black brassieres.

Whenever you see—or hear of—a single snowflake, you race to the grocery store for a panic-buy of bread, milk and beer.

YOU'RE A CHARLOTTEAN IF...

You put your bumper stickers on the paint.

You can shoot for the loot and not go to jail for it.

You (assuming you are Jewish) greet newcomers with "Shalom Y'all!"

You're considering a contribution to the bronze statue of Hugh Pharr McManaway, the town character who delighted—or terrified—drivers when he directed busy intersection traffic with a napkin.

You used to believe Jim and Tammy Bakker gave Charlotte some good exposure.

YOU'RE A CHARLOTTEAN IF...

You see nothing strange about wearing top hats with high tops.

You don't even consider it odd that two County Commissioners would publicly spar in a ring.

Televised City Council meetings, you believe, give new meaning to "trash TV."

You think John Boy and Billy are funny.

YOU'RE A LONGTIME CHARLOTTEAN IF...

Been There, Done That, Stuck Around

Now you don't have to be an "old timer" to be a "longtimer" around here, but your perspective is definitely different. Have you crossed the line between newcomer and longtimer? Here's how to find out. You're a longtime Charlottean if...

You haven't a clue how to drive in snow.

You still call Lake Wylie "the rivah."

You say "thank you" to store clerks who take your money.

YOU'RE A LONGTIME CHARLOTTEAN IF...

You let people merge into traffic in front of you.

You still believe in the fatherhood of God, the brotherhood of man and the neighborhood of Myers Park.

You assume that the Charlotte City Club is where public officials, influential businessmen and bankers *really* make those important city decisions.

You don't want to admit that, if it came down to a battle between the home boys and the transplants, history would likely repeat itself.

You know people who wax nostalgic about living in Piedmont Courts.

YOU'RE A LONGTIME CHARLOTTEAN IF...

You contend that the only thing better than Krispy Kremes was Spoon's ice cream.

You can't believe that people go uptown *at night!*

You remember when Bruton Smith didn't have any money.

You recall when Peter Gilchrist was *not* District Attorney.

You ever got married in York, South Carolina.

Until recently, you never got lost in a maze called a hospital.

YOU'RE A LONGTIME CHARLOTTEAN IF...

Before women's lib, you enjoyed the Queens College maypole tradition.

A fun "family outing" meant window-shopping at Ivey's and Belk's and snacking at the Kress lunch counter.

You sniffed your way along North Tryon from Montaldo's perfume (puffed from blowers around their doorway) to Woolworth's popcorn.

You are unaffected by street-name changes; you just don't pay attention to them.

You remember when they said that Sharon Amity was too far out to put the belt road.

YOU'RE A LONGTIME CHARLOTTEAN IF...

You went to school around the corner from home and respected your teacher.

You can do the Fred Kirby wave (put the back of your hand under your chin and wiggle your fingers).

You built your own car *with no motor* and raced it on a city street—in a Soapbox Derby.

You threw the *Charlotte Observer, News* or *Afro-American* in people's bushes.

You attended a wrestling match with your Sunday school class (!) on Wednesday night and watched yourself on WBTV the following Saturday.

YOU'RE A LONGTIME CHARLOTTEAN IF...

The worst trouble you ever got into at school was for chewing gum or talking.

You ever got threatened to be sent to Jackson Training School.

You used the odor from Bowater as a weather vane.

You could pick up the telephone book in one hand.

Before the annual Queen City Classic (Second Ward Tigers vs. West Charlotte Lions football game), you consumed your opponents.*

* The Friday before the game, the cafeteria at Second Ward would serve Lion Soup; West Charlotte cooked up Tiger Soup.

YOU'RE A LONGTIME CHARLOTTEAN IF...

When you went "brown bagging" before November, 1978, you were *not* grocery shopping.

You were among the crowd of fewer than 2,000 at a Mallard Creek Barbecue.

You paid to see Jerry Ball play a piano in a big glass case buried beneath the Park Road Shopping Center parking lot.

You've heard Ernest Johnson play the spinet organ on Memorial Hospital's 8th floor.

You joked that NCNB on the new skyscraper meant "Not Cutter's New Building."

YOU'RE A LONGTIME CHARLOTTEAN IF...

You discovered that the first overstreet walkway was not wheelchair-accessible.

You watched the most entertaining show on TV in the early '70s, the one that had drama, comedy and violence every week: the Charlotte-Mecklenburg School Board Meeting.

You saw the Charlotte-Mecklenburg school superintendent get fired on live TV (August, 1976).

In the spring and summer, you knew to look for the city's most gorgeous roses at places of business.*

* Avant Fuel & Ice Company (McGill Rose Garden), R.H. Bouligny, Inc. or the Rowe Building

YOU'RE A LONGTIME CHARLOTTEAN IF...

You were a tree-hugger before it was politically correct. (Remember South Wendover Road?)

Depending on your age, you women knew how to give a socially correct luncheon: by serving Mrs. Pressley's or Ludie's sandwiches.

Meanwhile, you guys knew how to party, too: you were crossing the state line to buy firewater and firecrackers in Fort Mill, South Carolina.

You tried out your long lens camera or binoculars spying on Thompson's Bootery & Bloomery (where they sold Buster Brown shoes and "bustin' out bikini" lingerie).

60

YOU'RE A LONGTIME CHARLOTTEAN IF...

A Way, Way, Way Backer!

Okay, some people can see further into the past than others. You know you're a lonnngtime Charlottean if...

You knew the most famous queen who ever lived in Charlotte: Ma Paxton, the bootleg queen who reigned from the '20s to the '50s and raised three beauty queen daughters on her profits.

You remember that during the mid-'30s, officers would pour homemade "rot gut" liquor down a floor drain at the police station, and thirsty residents would catch it flowing out a storm drain under a Sugaw Creek bridge.

YOU'RE A LONGTIME CHARLOTTEAN IF...

Your daddy or your granddad bought roasted peanuts from Old Man Lance at Griffith Park.

Your family went "to town" to go food shopping: at Pender's, Morris & Barnes and Charlotte Fish & Oyster. Or your groceries were delivered from Reid's.

In the '30s, you rode the only escalator south of Philadelphia, a wood-slat one in Efird's Department Store.

Your dad frequented Hice-Williamson Cigar Company, not for cigars nor the 35-cent lunch but to join the gamblers checking the balcony ticker tape for ball game scores and boxing match results.

YOU'RE A LONGTIME CHARLOTTEAN IF...

You believe that, until recently, Charlotte *never* had a trolley; we called them streetcars, although the electric P & N train between Charlotte and Gastonia was nicknamed the "Toonerville Trolley."

Your favorite sport was hill climbs on motorcycles at King's Mountain. (With a crowd watching, you'd roar up and fall down, but someone would lasso your cycle to keep it from crashing down the mountain).

You (if you're female) resented being allowed to visit the City Club via the women's entrance only. If you're male, you saw nothing wrong with that.

You participated in drag races vs. bootleggers during the '40s—like say from Green Gables, the Myers Park hangout, down Providence Road.

YOU'RE A LONGTIME CHARLOTTEAN IF...

You swam at the Y.M.C.A. when they did not *allow* you to wear a swimming suit.

You went skinny dipping in Briar Creek.

Arthur Smith and the Crackerjacks were the greatest celebrities you knew.

You grocery shopped at Harris, when there was no Teeter, no deli and no sushi.

You paid a dime or a token to ride a city bus operated by Duke Power.

You used to dodge cows on Highway 51.

YOU'RE A LONGTIME CHARLOTTEAN IF...

You can recall when Wendover Road marked the city limits and the end of the bus line and...

> beyond Highway 49 were trees,
> beyond Idlewild Road was "the boonies,"
> beyond Highway 51, Outer Mongolia.

You never had to leave home before sunrise to get to work on time.

You saw "Sweet Daddy Grace's" long fingernails in person.

Either Sam or Peter had something to do with your birth.*

* You were born in Good Samaritan Hospital, known as "Good Sam" or at St. Peter's Hospital, both located uptown.

YOU'RE A LONGTIME CHARLOTTEAN IF...

You're still referring to the Bank of America as American Trust.

The most recognizable public voices you recall were not those of politicians but of Grady Cole, Genial Gene Potts, Chatty Hatty and Jimmy Kilgo.

The most scandalous event of your teen years happened during the Olympic Civinettes' initiation ritual of jumping off Withers Bridge: a girl lost her bra.

You drank milkshakes at the Boar's Head Drive-In and parked at the "Pearly Gates"* or started out at Babe Maloy's and ended up at "Harbor Lights"**

*Gates to a subdivision that never was, located between McAlway and Canterbury Roads
** A favorite make-out spot near the runway lights of the old Charlotte airport

YOU'RE A LONGTIME CHARLOTTEAN IF...

You used to order a timber float (toothpick in a glass of water) and make tomato juice out of water and ketchup for a free outing at the Town House.

You were less of a consumer—not exactly by choice: most stores were not open on Wednesday or Saturday afternoons nor on Sundays. Banks closed at 1 p.m.

As a child, you and the other neighborhood kids ran after the trucks spewing white clouds of DDT to kill mosquitos.

You attended Hornets' BASEBALL games (football, too!).

You called Grier or McEwen Funeral Home for an emergency ambulance.

YOU'RE A LONGTIME CHARLOTTEAN IF...

Your idea of a swell dinner date was at Ingram's El Chico or Oscar Harris' Sandwich Shop on South McDowell or Fred Kemp's Cafe on East Second Street.

You remember when Officer 'Bub' Houston walked a beat around Brooklyn near First and McDowell for many years and never shot anyone.

You participated in the '50s version of the "snipe hunt": sitting in a car "necking" in front of the huge Allied Van sign on West Morehead Street, awaiting the midnight hour, when the driver supposedly would get out to change a tire. Of course, "nice girls" had an 11 p.m. curfew, so no one ever saw him.

You can't forget the newspaper article about Elvis Presley's Charlotte visit that reported how he fingered a waitress's slip.

69

YOU'RE A LONGTIME CHARLOTTEAN IF...

You approved of J. B. Ivey's interpretation of the 4th Commandment (covering his department store display windows on Sundays).

You wondered why they called that stinky midtown creek "Sugar" until you found out that (despite the sign-maker's version), it bore the Indian name "Sugaw."

Long before desegregation, you stood and ate side by side with people of the other race at Tanner's (a hot-dog-orange-juice-and-peanuts bar) practicing what Harry Golden called "vertical integration."

You found out from experience that our grand new coliseum with the largest unsupported dome in the world was a roaster oven with no air conditioning.

YOU'RE A LONGTIME CHARLOTTEAN IF...

You joined the search for Vicki, the elephant that escaped from the Airport Park on Wilkinson Boulevard and eluded search parties and helicopters for days.

Whenever you came out of Rone's Lunch, you waved to the Tin Man on top of Daughtry's Sheet Metal Company.

You used to wonder what good the disinfectant foot wash did at Suttle's Swim Club, when the rest of the place smelled so bad.

You attended the grand opening of Charlottetown Mall (now Midtown Square) when they buried a time "capsule," which was really a child's burial vault.*

* Actually, it was vault #2. Someone was checking to see how it worked before the ceremony and closed the top, accidently sealing it. They had to rush out and buy a new one.

YOU'RE A LONGTIME CHARLOTTEAN IF...

Leroy Crane, the elevator captain at the Johnson Building, called you by name.

When you refer to "the old airport," you mean the one at Tuckaseegee and Ashley Roads.

You called A.G. Junior High "Ancient Garbage" during its last decade on the site of the present Central Y.M.C.A.

You could have told those New Yorkers 40 years ago that Krispy Kremes were to ordinary doughnuts like angels are to ordinary people.

You knew a few turkeys who *didn't* live at Morrocroft Farm.

YOU'RE A NEWCOMER IF...

New Kids on the Block

We can usually spot you with our ears or our eyes, but we want you to know that we have a lot in common, especially our affection for the Queen City. And we've one request: shhhh, don't tell anyone else! Meanwhile, you know you're a newcomer if...

You think red clay is pretty.

When someone says "Y'all come over sometime," you actually go.

When you ask for tea in a restaurant, you assume it will be hot.

YOU'RE A NEWCOMER IF...

You assumed Queen Charlotte was British and beautiful. (See her portrait at the Mint Museum. She was born in Mecklenburg-Strelitz, Germany and is ugh... ugh...ugly.)

You've discovered that every day, not just Wednesdays, here is hump day. Proof: drive down Barclay Downs Drive, Laurel Avenue or Billingsley Road.

You think that traffic really isn't so bad here.

You want to know about the founder of the Mint Museum, Mr. Mint.

You hide your car on Sundays so your neighbors will think you're at church.

YOU'RE A NEWCOMER IF...

You are surprised when your sandwich from Price's Chicken Coop is two pieces of bread with a thigh inside—bone and all.

You thought Scots-Irish was a drink with an identity problem.

You've planted some of that lush kudzu as a ground cover for your garden.

You believe I-77's Exit 25 is in the country.

You question the idea of giving a theater the last name of the guy who assassinated Lincoln *in a theater*.

YOU'RE A NEWCOMER IF...

You're amazed to hear macho men talking about paper dolls.

The first thing you did when you got here was learn to crawl—pub crawl that is.

You've already found out where to be which night to meet interesting people.

You're more up-to-date on the best entertainment spots in town than the natives.

You don't take for granted our culture, our diversity and our beautiful trees.

YOU'RE A NEWCOMER IF...

These Take Some 'Splainin.'

1. You wonder who this Sharon girl is and who she's sleeping with.

2. You ask for bed and breakfast at Hotel Charlotte.

3. You assume B. T. stands for a Honeybee's t-shirt.

4. You spend time hunting for the Belmont Tunnel.

5. You think the local Navajos are Indians.

YOU'RE A NEWCOMER IF...

6. You try to join the Belle Acres Golf & Country Club to play tennis or 18 holes of golf.

7. Although you knew that Charlotte is famous for its trees, you were amazed to hear that the city has a rain forest.

8. You can't find that parking garage, Meck Dec.

9. You can't believe that people of normal intelligence took six years to get through Myers Park High School.

10. You balk at going to a florist for supper.

YOU'RE A NEWCOMER IF...

The 'Splainin'

1. It was a rural community with a Presbyterian Church bearing the biblical name Sharon.

2. This "speakeasy" has a fake hotel lobby and guest room doors from the old Charlotte Hotel, but no beds—and no food before 11:45 a.m.

3. It's what we call the city's first radio station, which has only three call letters: WBT.

4. That's a mythical place known only to former Charlotte deejay, Bill Curry, but a popular "insiders" joke.

5. Dating from Central High's dance club days, this men's social club still meets monthly. Most members are in their 80s and 90s.

YOU'RE A NEWCOMER IF...

6. Pronounced Belly Ache-ers, this members-only club is a tongue-in-cheek restaurant, bar and party place, with plenty of games to play. They *used to* have table tennis and miniature golf. Now, they feature a golf pinball machine and an indoor pool (table).

7. There is one at Discovery Place, the hands-on science museum.

8. That's our slang term for the Mecklenburg Declaration of Independence, a missing document written in 1775. On May 20, we celebrate "Meck Dec" Day.

9. The school opened in 1951 for grades 7-12.

10. The Ratcliffe Florist sign still hangs in front of Carpe Diem Restaurant.

HEAD SCRATCHERS

Just Wondering...

If Charlotte is such a great place to live, how come so many people leave on the weekends?

How did Richardson & Company come up with the name Panthers, a non-indigenous animal? More appropriate: Junk Yard Dogs (the stadium property, you know, is the site of Swartz's junk yard).

Why was the landmark JFG sign with its twinkling lights hazardous to traffic but the new Duke Energy neon sculpture is not?

HEAD SCRATCHERS

What would YOU put on a newly designed city flag? Trees? Or cars? Try counting both from an uptown skyscraper.

Who decided to call the Hornets cheerleaders Honeybees instead of Hornettes?

How can it be that so many people who built expensive houses in Airlie are native Charlotteans who *knew* it was a flood plain?

If we're not yet a world class city, how come the Open Kitchen has been "world famous" and Anderson's has had the "world's best" pecan pie for decades?

QUEENZ QUIZ

Try This!

Did you pass the test to fit the profile of a typical Charlottean? Here's a way to win bonus points. Answer these correctly and you're eligible to wear a crown.

Charlotte is known as the Queen City because...

A. It's the home of Queens College.
B. It was named for George III's wife, Queen Charlotte.
C. Drag queens preen and perform around town on a nightly basis.
D. All of the above.

QUEENZ QUIZ

Nectar of the gods around these parts is...

    A. Sweetened iced tea.
    B. Budweiser.
    C. Cheerwine.
    D. All of the above.

Although no "cow town," Charlotte has been the home of one or more well-known cowboys, such as:

    A. Fred Kirby
    B. Randolph Scott
    C. Coyote Joe
    D. Texas Pete

QUEENZ QUIZ

The only time the Honeybees ever wore skimpy red outfits was to...

    A. Celebrate Christmas and Valentine's Day
    B. Be bridesmaids at a halftime wedding
    C. Tease the Bulls
    D. Volunteer for the fire department

The Southeast's largest country club, according to the owners, is located in the Queen City. It is:

    A. Charlotte Country Club
    B. Quail Hollow Country Club
    C. Belle Acres Country Club
    D. Coyote Joe's

QUEENZ QUIZ

The city's seal has a predominant symbol. It is a...

     A. Hornet's nest, because the Revolutionary War general, Cornwallis, called Charlotte a "hornets' nest of rebellion."

     B. Stylized crown to signify that this is the Queen City.

     C. Gold brick, because the first gold rush in America was here, and there are lots of "gold brickers" around.

     D. Orange and white traffic barrel, the predominant sight seen by motorists.

YOU'RE CONSIDERED A NATIVE IF...

The *real* test:

You've been here a full year.

Contributor's Form

Ideas for some great lines for Volume 2 of:

YOU CAN TELL YOU'RE A CHARLOTTEAN IF...

You're a Charlottean If..._____

_____

You're a Longtime Charlottean If.. _____

_____

You're a Newcomer If.. _____

_____

Head Scratcher _____

_____

Queenz Quiz_____

_____

Idea for a new feature: _____

_____

_____

_____

Contributor's name_____

Address_____**Phone**_____

City _____**State/Zip**_____

Please mail this form to: **A. Borough Books**
P.O. Box 15391
Charlotte, NC 28211

Contributor's Form

Ideas for some great lines for Volume 2 of:

YOU CAN TELL YOU'RE A CHARLOTTEAN IF...

You're a Charlottean If..._____

_____

You're a Longtime Charlottean If.. _____

_____

You're a Newcomer If.. _____

_____

Head Scratcher _____

_____

Queenz Quiz_____

_____

Idea for a new feature: _____

_____

_____

_____

Contributor's name_____

Address_____**Phone**_____

City _____**State/Zip**_____

Please mail this form to: **A. Borough Books**
P.O. Box 15391
Charlotte, NC 28211

Order Form

Please complete both sides of this form

_____copies of *You Can Tell You're a Charlottean If...*@ $7.95 _____

Postage and handling $2 for first 2; 50¢ each additional copy _____

NC residents must pay 6% tax (48¢ for one) _____

TOTAL _____

Personalized as a gift for _____

His/her relationship to Charlotte_____

Name_____

Address_____**Phone**_____

City _____**State/Zip**_____

Other humor books by ABB:

_____copies of *Gray-Haired Grins & Giggles* - "Senior Humor"

  True-experience tales by 45 senior authors. 128 pages

  standard print: $12.95 large print(144 pages): $13.95 _____

_____ copies of *You've GOT to Have a Sense of Humor to*

  Have a Wedding - Bigger, Margaret G. 128 pages

  True wedding tales - humorous, disastrous, outrageous

  Plus advice not found in wedding guides. $9.95 _____

  NO EXTRA POSTAGE if you buy a Charlotte book

  NC residents must pay 6% state tax _____

  TOTAL _____

Send check or money order to: **A. Borough Books**
  P.O. Box 15391
  Charlotte, NC 28211